Marriage has been the vessel by which I have come to know my Lord, and He gets all praise, glory and honor. I would like to dedicate this book to my **husband,** *W.S. Lee. He promised over 50 years ago, I would not be bored – he has more than kept his promise. Our journey through life has become, The Reason Is....*

THE REASON IS...

Published by
Watersprings Media House, LLC.
P.O. Box 1284
Olive Branch, MS 38654
www.waterspringsmedia.com
For permission requests and bulk orders contact publisher.
Copyrights © 2018 Wilma Kirk Lee. All rights reserved.

No part of this publication may be reproduced, distributed, or transmitted in any form or by any means, including photocopying, recording, or other electronic or mechanical methods, without the prior written permission of the publisher, except in the case of brief quotations embodied in critical reviews and certain other noncommercial uses permitted by copyright law.

Scripture quotations marked "ESV" are taken from *The Holy Bible, English Standard Version.* Copyright © 2000; 2001 by Crossway Bibles, a division of Good News Publishers. Used by permission. All rights reserved.

Scripture taken from the *New American Standard Bible*, © Copyright 1960, 1962, 1968, 1971, 1973, 1975, 1977 by the Lockman Foundation. Used by permission.

Scripture quotations are taken from the *Holy Bible, New International Version*®. NIV® Copyright 1973, 1978, 1984 by International Bible Society. Used by permission of Zondervan. All rights reserved.

Scripture quotations marked "NKJV" are taken from the *New King James Version.* Copyright © 1982 by Thomas Nelson, Inc. Used by permission. All rights reserved.

Scripture quotations marked (NLT) are taken from the *Holy Bible, New Living Translation,* copyright © 1996. Used by permission of Tyndale House Publishers, Inc., Wheaton, IL 60189 USA. All rights reserved.

Scripture quotations from *THE MESSAGE.* Copyright © by Eugene H. Peterson 1993, 1994, 1995, 1996, 2000, 2001, 2002. Used by permission of NavPress Publishing Group.

Printed in the United States of America.
Library of Congress Control Number: 2018960048
ISBN-13: 978-1-948877-05-3

The Reason Is...

by

Wilma Kirk Lee

Table of Contents

Prologue 5

Chapter 1: A Lifetime Not A Day.................... 9

Chapter 2: Recipes Change, Principles Last ... 14

Chapter 3: Priorities.. 19

Chapter 4: Can We Laugh With Each Other?. 24

Test Your HQ (HumorQuotient)..................... 27

Chapter 5: What? I Don't Get Everything I Want? (Flexibility) 34

Chapter 6:
Hey! I Married YOU – Not Your Family! 38

Chapter 7: Becoming One 44

Chapter 8: The Journey Continues… 50

AUTHOR BIO 57

The Reason Is...

Prologue

I write not as an expert, but as one of two people who have seen the journey be joyful and full through the years that we have been joined together. We know that the Lord has been a part of our relationship; we could not have come this far together if He weren't the Head of this marriage. We've shared our tears and disagreements, but the joys and laughter have far outweighed the tears. We're still growing and enjoying the trip.

This book has its beginnings with a trip to Andrews Seventh-day Adventist University in Berrien Springs, Michigan in 1976. We had planned to attend a Family Life Conference. We had no idea what we were getting ourselves into, certainly a book was the farthest thing from our mind. During that conference, we were introduced to many marriage strengthening modalities, and we realized there might be a wider area for ministry than we realized. We were a pastoral couple with three young children. I had made careful plans for the children, because this was to be a "get-away" for us as a couple, as well as a learning experience, we would just have time for the two of us. However, that was not to be the case - we had the youngest with us, she was two at the time! It was a challenge to make meetings that began at 8:00AM and sometimes lasted until 9:00PM with a toddler in tow. Yet, it was a great awakening for our relationship as a couple, as parents, and for me as an individual!

Some months later, we experienced our first marriage retreat with Ed and Letah Banks which will remain etched in our memory for the remarkable effect it had upon us and our relationship. That weekend started us on a path with marriage that we knew was too good to keep to ourselves. This book is one of the ways we can share the good news of marriage with others.

When I was a child, my Father often said, "Cheap thing no good; good thing no cheap."

Marriage falls into that category. A good marriage requires a lot of work, but it is well worth the investment. I find that out every day, and it's so much fun!

Now on to some principles for making your marriage a unique reflection of God's glory. Each marriage is a unique opportunity to reflect God's love – appropriate since God created EACH of us as His masterpiece Ephesians 2:10 (AMP) *For we are His workmanship [His own master work, a work of art], created in Christ Jesus [reborn from above— spiritually transformed, renewed, ready to be used] for good works....*

A sense of commitment, regardless of the circumstances, will make the difference in a relationship worth extending oneself. Being willing to take the risk of being vulnerable, or not always having things go exactly the way you want because the marriage relationship is the most important thing. Commitment will cause two people to stop and realize that what they have together is too precious to throw away. They will be willing to work together and negotiate to make their relationship what it could be.

For me, commitment means moving, more times than I **ever** imagined a family could ever relocate. Moving is not one of my favorite things to do, in fact, it's the reason I said, "***I will never marry a preacher!***" God has such a delightful sense of humor! The man He sent into my life **is** a preacher. I have had the privilege of living all over the United States, with the exception of the Northwest. After the initial trauma of packing is over, I can say it has truly been an adventure. I have learned so much and made many friends. I should not have been surprised. When my husband proposed he asked, "Do you think you could spend the rest of your life with me without being bored?" **CLUE!!!!!!!**

Chapter 1

A Lifetime

Not A Day

The Reason Is...

*When I look back on all the years - Remembering the joy
and the tears. Maybe this is the reason we're together.
God gave us children and they grew
And every day our love did too
Maybe this is the reason we're together.
For the reason is not who we are,
or what we've done to come this far,
The reason is not all the steps we've trod. But we've kept
our eyes on God's Dear Son,
And we praise Him for this lasting love.
We both know, the Reason is God!
© Gale Jones Murphy 08/30/91*

Unless the Lord builds a house, the work of the

builders is wasted. (Psalm 127:1 NLT). The words seem so simple, however, in reality the task is difficult to begin and definitely difficult to complete. In the first glow of new love, there is not a thing that two people would not do to make each other happy and comfortable. They want to spend each and every moment together and the "beloved" is perfect. For some, reality comes earlier than others – the challenge of dealing with a mortal who has both assets and liabilities is the basis for a relationship that can stand the test of time.

It seems that everyone thinks that there is a magic formula that will make everything work out all right, and provide for the *happily ever after* ending. However, one of the things that happens with life is that things don't always come to a neat ending. There are some things that cannot be *"fixed"* or completely resolved. Thus, it is important to determine that no matter what the situation, both partners are committed to the relationship with each other for a lifetime.

A sense of **commitment,** regardless of the

circumstances will make the difference between how much work should be invested into a lifelong friendship. Two components of a lifelong friendship are vulnerability and flexibility. **Commitment** will cause two people to stop and realize what they have together is too precious to throw away. They will be willing to communicate and negotiate to make their relationship what it should be.

Commitment leads to two major skills that lead to a long marriage: **communication** and **forgiveness.** Most people feel they communicate: *they talk well.* However, the greatest skill of communication is **LISTENING.** The dictionary defines listening as *to hear something with thoughtful attention: give consideration.* Today's society bursting with social media does not require listening, just sharing words!

The transition from single to married brings many changes and listening tops the list. I remember during the days of my courtship, we spent many HOURS on the telephone. We were separated during our year, two months and two days of engagement, so our frequent phone calls were a highly anticipated event. I learned to listen because that was an opportunity to get to know this person I was planning to spend the rest of my life with.

Of course, I had no idea I still didn't know that much about listening. I have since learned that listening requires not just the words, but the tone of voice and most importantly, nonverbals. Nonverbals are those things that are shared through: eye contact, proximity, touch. Listening requires full attention, not distraction; think about the times you've committed to something you didn't want to do because you were distracted when you responded. By the way, another thing I learned was if the words and tone of voice do not match the nonverbals, I should believe the nonverbals.

One of the other important things I learned – no mind-reading. You know, mind reading when you finish the other person's sentence BEFORE

The Reason Is...

they stop speaking! Listening means allowing the other person to completely express themselves, and then when a response is made, make certain you're responding to what was meant. Listening requires committed TIME!

Chapter 2

Recipes Change, Principles Last

> *So, chosen by God for this new life of love, dress in the wardrobe God picked out for you: compassion, kindness, humility, quiet strength, discipline. Be even-tempered, content with second place, quick to forgive an offense. Forgive as quickly and completely as the Master forgave you. And regardless of what else you put on, wear love. It's your basic, all-purpose garment. Never be without it.*
> *Colossians 3:12-14 (MSG)*

If you have a cookbook dated in the 1930's - 1950's, you might find recipe titles that look familiar, but some of the listed ingredients might appear strange! The general principle for creating the dish may remain the same, but during that time-period some of the things weren't even available: stand mixer, blender, food processor, microwave oven, to name a few. No one today is perplexed by the difference in recipes – the question is – what will the food taste like when this recipe is completed?

Today, the recipe for building a marriage has changed. Some people live together prior to getting married; others just live together and state there is no need for a marriage ceremony. The discomfort with commitment means there are those who choose not to have a relationship without any *strings!* Each person is free to do whatever makes them happy.

The principle for marriage is a spiritual one. In Genesis 2:20-25 (AMP) … *but for Adam there was not found a helper [that was] suitable (a companion) for him. So the Lord God caused a deep sleep to fall upon Adam; and while he slept, He took one of his ribs and closed up the flesh at that place. And the rib which the Lord God had taken from the man He made (fashioned, formed) into a woman, and He brought her and presented her to the man. Then Adam said, "This is now bone of my bones, And flesh of my flesh; She shall be called Woman, Because she was taken out of Man."* For this reason, a man shall leave his father and his mother, and shall be joined to his wife; and they shall become one flesh. And the man and his wife were both naked and were not ashamed or embarrassed.

The first marriage ever performed was by God! He provides some specific principles for marriage going forward:

- Leave father and mother
- Be joined together
- Become one flesh

The principle has not changed, listen to what the Lord says, *"I am God—yes, I Am. I haven't changed.* Malachi 3:6 (MSG). I know, some will say that's in the Old Testament. Let's see what the Lord has to say about permanence in the New Testament: Revelation 22:13 (AMP) *"I am the Alpha and the Omega, the First and the Last, the Beginning and the End [the Eternal One]."*

Since God created marriage, He gets the final word, and He says He hasn't changed. So, His principles upon which marriage is based have not changed. Current society may attempt to adapt the recipe, but the results will not resemble the original recipe.

The foundation for a marriage with your friend depends upon the friendship you have with God. He loves us; He created us; He redeemed us, and His plan is that we have only the best. We have to develop a personal relationship with our Creator-Redeemer first. We must believe He created us in **HIS** image, He will not withhold anything that will bless and benefit us if we follow Him in love. Besides, if you are in a friendship with the Lord, HE will talk to you about your other friendship choices. He will definitely speak to a friend you plan to spend the rest of your life with.

It's easy to talk Christian talk – all you need is the right vocabulary! It's not easy to live the Christian life on a daily basis. Remember, the person you are planning to spend the rest of your life with will also be the one who may squeeze the toothpaste in the middle of the tube and offer burnt toast – you fill in the blanks. What will your life be like on a daily basis if one or both of you are pretending to be a Christian?

Remember the clothing spoken of at the beginning of this chapter: the wardrobe God picked out for you: compassion, kindness, humility, quiet strength, discipline…even-tempered, content with second place, quick to forgive an offense…. This is what you need to check in your own closet first, then in the closet of the one with whom you plan to spend your life. If the clothing is not present during courtship, it won't magically appear **after** you're married!

Principles are valuable and lasting – they are the foundation of **commitment**!

Chapter 3

Priorities

Live life, then, with a due sense of responsibility, not as men who do not know the meaning and purpose of life but as those who do. Make the best use of your time, despite all the difficulties of these days.
Ephesians 5:15-16 (PHILLIPS)

Time, time, and more time will always have a place in a committed marriage. It is easy to get caught up in the demands of life and family and take for granted the presence of the person to whom you have committed your life to. The intention that was made during courtship and the early stages of the relationship must be preset to make certain nothing interferes with the time spent as a couple.

When children become a part of the family, they learn they are not always a part of parental activity. It isn't easy! Yet, nothing in life worth having is ever easy. It also provides a valuable lesson in empathy for children when they learn they are NOT the center of the universe.

One of the special times in our marriage was the wonderful gift our children provided when they helped us go away for a New Year's celebration. They were all pre-teens, and we were pleasantly surprised to learn they appreciated our couple-ness, even then.

We were told, "We have spoken with our NY grandparents and they are planning for us to spend New Year's with them, so you can do something as a couple. We think you need to have some time away from us just for the two of you!" We were speechless.

Today, after all of our children are launched, and we are now home alone again, it's still a challenge to have time that is specific to us as a couple. I don't think we're alone with attempting

The Reason Is...

to set priority in our marriage relationship along with all of our other responsibilities.

Consider this:

> *Imagine there is a bank account that credits your account each morning with $86,400. It carries over no balance from day to day.*
>
> *Every evening the bank deletes whatever part of the balance you failed to use during the day. What would you do? Draw out every cent, of course?*
>
> *Each of us has such a bank. Its name is **TIME**. Every morning, it credits you with 86,400 seconds. Every night it writes off as lost, whatever of this you have failed to invest to a good purpose. It carries over no balance. It allows no overdraft. Each day it opens a new account for you. Each night it burns the remains of the day.*
>
> *If you fail to use the day's deposits, the loss is yours. There is no drawing against "tomorrow." You must live in the present on today's deposits. Invest it so as to get from it the utmost in health, happiness and success! The clock is running!*

Treasure every moment that you have! And treasure it more because you shared it with someone special, special enough to spend your time with. And remember time waits for no one. – Yesterday is history. Tomorrow is a mystery. Today is a gift. That's why it's called the present.

The presence of media, phones, tablets, etc., in our lives today is a subtle challenge to our time. It's difficult to determine how much time we actually spend involved with the "others" of media, and the impact media has on our face-to-face relationships. US adults spend an average of 1 hour, 16 minutes each day watching video on digital devices. (Pew Reports, Demographics of Media 2018).

A marriage that lacks intimate time is a marriage with trouble on the horizon! A personal investment in committed time is necessary to have a marriage that lasts throughout the ages. Two people cannot spend time elsewhere and expect to have a vibrant marriage.

The next time you are out at dinner or some other public place, look around and note the people who are sitting with each other and using media to connect with someone who is not present! I remember going to a restaurant with my husband. We noted a couple who were seated across from us. The young woman was on her phone when they were seated, throughout the meal, and when it was time for the check. She asked for her food to be boxed because she had been on the phone **the entire time!** I must admit, I was amazed the young man chose to pay for the meal!

The best advice given for setting priorities was written by Solomon: "Enjoy the wife you married as a young man! Lovely as an angel, beautiful as a rose—don't ever quit taking delight in her body. Never take her love for granted!" Proverbs 5:18 (MSG)

Chapter 4

Can We Laugh With Each Other?

But the time is coming when you're going to hear laughter and celebration, marriage festivities, people exclaiming, "Thank God-of-the-Angel-Armies. He's so good! His love never quits...." (Jeremiah 33:11 MSG)

A sense of humor is an important factor in a relationship that stands the test of time. Life is truly serious, yet most of us take ourselves too seriously. Laughter and joy is an ingredient that is missing in too many hearts and homes today.

Memories are the process of a lifetime. One of the main components of memories is laughter.

The Reason Is...

When people look back on the major commitment of their life, a smile and delight comes to their faces and eyes.

One of the interesting quotes attributed to the late, Barbara Bush was *"I married George because he made me laugh."* It's obvious that laughter was a factor in their 73-year marriage. They were the longest married presidential couple in history! It was always interesting to see them together; their faces were always pleasant, and they were looking at each other.

What is the humor quotient of **your** marriage? Does the mere thought of your spouse bring a smile to your face? Are your memories laced with laughter? If not, it's not too late to begin a new routine. What would make your spouse laugh?

Just to be sure, there is a difference between laughing *at* and laughing **with**. Sometimes cutting sarcasm is used as a *put-down* of the other person in the relationship. That's laughing *at* the other person.

Of course, the Bible tells us, *"A happy heart is*

good medicine and a joyful mind causes healing...." Proverbs 17:22 (AMP). It is difficult in our world today to have a joyful mind, and when we consider all the challenges of married life: intimate relationships, children, finances, and all the rest, it would be easy to just allow circumstances to determine our attitude and altitude. Marriages that stand the test of time are full of joy.

Research tells us, the minimum number of laughs needed per day by adults is 30. Change this to at least 100 and recognize that the sky is the limit. *(Beck, Martha, PhD. The Joy Diet. p 160-*

162. NY: Crown Publishers, 2003.)

Laughter is free! It's a shame we don't avail ourselves of it more.

I remember a time quite a few years ago, my husband and I were traveling with some young people. The trip covered a few days by car, so we had gotten to know our fellow travelers rather well. One of them commented that my husband and I laughed a lot together; they found that a bit strange. We explained to them it was a part of our

The Reason Is...

relationship - laughter **with** each other not **at** each other.

Here's a quiz to test your **HQ** (**Humor Quotient**). See where you land on the scale, and then think about how this impacts your marriage.

Test Your HQ
(Humor Quotient)

1. **When I make a mistake**

    a) I laugh and see what I can learn from the experience

    b) I beat myself up

    c) I blame the government

2. **When my schedule is extremely busy**

    a) I keep my nose to the grindstone

    b) I occasionally take a break to relax and have fun

    c) I hire an actor who looks like me to appear

at family dinners

3. When I tell a joke, people:

a) laugh

b) groan

c) report me to the harassment board

4. I forget to laugh

a) when I'm really busy

b) when I'm at a comedy club

c) when my toast lands on the floor -- butter side down

5. I plan to reward myself with fun and relaxation:

a) each day

b) only on weekends and holidays

c) when cloning becomes affordable

The Reason Is...

6.　People view me:

a)　as a serious person

b)　as a light-hearted person on occasion

c)　as so funny I should be banned from visiting the hospital hernia unit

7.　The key people in my life

a)　are fun-loving

b)　are happy only during happy hour

c)　now all have unlisted phone numbers

8.　Making people laugh

a)　comes easily to me

b)　comes easily to me only if I steal other people's jokes

c)　comes easily to me, but unfortunately not on purpose

9. When I was growing up, my family:

a)   valued fun, laughter, humor and play

b)   were often afflicted with AADS (Acquired Amusement Deficiency Syndrome)

c)   made Spock look like a one-man carnival

Scoring

1. a.3 b.2 c.1

2. a.2 b.3 c.1

3. a.3 b.2 c.1

4. a.2 b.1 c.3

5. a.3 b.2 c.1

6. a.1 b.2 c.3

7. a.3 b.2 c.1

8. a.3 b.2 c.1

9. a.3 b.2 c.1

Total Score =

Results

If your score was 30 or more – put the whoopee cushion down! You live so much on the funny side of your brain that we might need to occasionally stimulate your "tax return" brain.

If your score was 25--29, you are grooving. You have a well-developed funny brain and a good balance of fun versus work ethic. It is normal to have some negativity – and actually, is necessary as a card-carrying human.

If your score was 20-24, get thee to a funnery! Your overly grave behavior will lead you—yes, you guessed it--to an early grave. Install the latest version of Mirth Manager 4.1 right away and delete Wet Blanket 3.2 immediately. Start by creating an area of your office just for fun stuff – a humor bulletin board, comedy CD's, games, etc.

If your score was under 19, you might want to get a T- shirt that says, "I am the Beacon of Doom" and look in the mirror. You need serious fun help. But don't worry (which I know is hard for you) because there is lots of help available; call us for more ideas or check out our web site for more articles.

Carla Rieger is the Director of The Artistry of Change. She speaks at conventions, sales rallies and appreciation events on how to turn workplace negativity into creativity -- unlocking your genius for outstanding performance. She has written three books including The Change Artist, The Power of Laughter, Speaking on the Funny Side of the Brain, and The Heart of Presenting.

The Reason Is...

Laughter is something in a marriage that **costs NOTHING!!!!** Often couples complain because everything costs something to develop the marriage. Laughter is a gift to all marriages that is free – an excellent investment for a lifetime. Here's a paraphrase to remember: "A marriage without a sense of humor is like a wagon without springs – jolted by every pebble in the road." The wisest man, Solomon, said it best – *"A cheerful heart brings a smile to your face; a sad heart makes it hard to get through the day."* Proverbs 15:13 (MSG)

Chapter 5

What? I Don't Get Everything I Want? (Flexibility)

Now let's talk about Christian freedom. As a Christian I'm a free man (woman), and in one sense I have a right to do what I want; but some of those things are not beneficial. In other words, things may be permissible but not constructive.
(1 Cor. 10:23, Clear Word)

It's important to realize: **No one gets EVERYTHING they want, ALL of the time!** Flexibility is a quality that makes a lengthy marriage, but it's difficult to achieve. We are all born wanting our own way.

In fact, during early childhood, young children

are noticeably *ego-centric*. A mark of maturity is the ability to realize that the world does not revolve around oneself, and that others and their needs must be considered as well.

Today's society has promoted the false message that **everyone** is **entitled** to privilege. Think about it: in elementary school sports, **all** participants get a trophy; graduation ceremonies boast **multiple** valedictorians; jobs must fulfill all one's needs – or they don't work! You get the picture.

When two people marry, they are to become a **TEAM,** not combatants. Yet, if the mindset is that each person will get everything they want all the time, this is not the groundwork for a successful team. This is a time when couples who have had pre-marriage as a part of their preparation may have an advantage. One of the tasks of pre-marriage is to give couples tools for the times when the "glow" begins to waver.

The Best textbook tells us, *"Accept life with humility and patience, making allowances for each other because you love each other." Ephesians 4:2(PHILLIPS)*. In the daily pace of life, sometimes humility, patience are not the qualities we want to manifest. We want what we want – **NOW!!!!**

Love for a lifetime helps us to remember that we are not in this relationship alone, and we must be considerate of how our partner is feeling. I realized early in our marriage, I'm married to a man who passes out *"round- to- its"*! He will do what is requested – when he gets around to it. Now, I'm the type of temperament when I ask for something, I want an immediate response. Needless to say, we had a problem.

When I realized one of the components of an intimate relationship was flexibility, then I began to realize I could not take receiving a *"round-to-it"* as an indicator or my husband's love for me, just his style. Marriage is the place where I am learning to put my Christian beliefs into practice. The text reminds me, I need ***humility, patience*** in abundance because by temperament that is not my strength. I have learned that when I am patient, my request is usually fulfilled.

I have also learned that God had a plan when He put us together. He meant to show how two people who are so different could become a team and reflect His glory. I knew we were on the way when we were told one day if we were both on a committee, we were a **MAJORITY**!

Flexibility isn't natural, and it isn't easy, but I can say from my personal experience – it's highly rewarding. It makes a lifetime of marriage interesting and exciting. It helps to fulfill the second greatest commandment: *"This is the second: 'You shall [unselfishly] [a]love your neighbor as yourself.' There is no other commandment greater than these."* Mark 12:31 (AMP). The key to understanding this and other statements about love is to know that this love (the Greek word agape) is not so much a matter of emotion as it is of doing things for the benefit of another person, that is, having an unselfish concern for another and a willingness to seek the best for another. This is truly a daily challenge, but one well worth taking.

Chapter 6

Hey! I Married YOU – Not Your Family!

This explains why a man leaves his father and mother and is joined to his wife, and the two are united into one. (Genesis 2:24 NLT)

Here's the challenge – we have lived with **our** families of origin all of our lives. We are starting a new family with someone who has lived with **their** families of origin all of their lives. Each family is different – even if they have lived in the same neighborhood and you have known each other all their lives!

The Reason Is...

There are few things I realized early in our marriage, separation is not easy, and it is difficult for both the newly married couple and the parents. Looking at the words of the Scripture above, I'm always surprised to realize that when God told Adam and Eve about leaving their father and mother, they didn't have either parent – they had been created by God! It took a while to realize that God was creating a principle of **boundaries** for those who marry after Adam and Eve.

Families are necessary. The role of a strong Christian family is to prepare children to become independent individuals who start their own families. The interesting thing about this process, parents have a very difficult time allowing their children to become their own person.

One of the explicit descriptions of boundaries in marriage is the following quote, "There is a sacred circle around every family which should be preserved. No other one has any right in that sacred circle.

"The husband and wife should be all to each other.

The wife should have no secrets to keep from her husband and let others know, and the husband should have no secrets to keep from his wife to relate to others. The heart of his wife should be the grave for the faults of the husband, and the heart of the husband the grave for his wife's faults.

Never should either party indulge in a joke at the expense of the other's feelings. Never should either the husband or wife in sport or in any other manner complain of each other to others, for frequently indulging in this foolish and what may seem perfectly harmless joking will end in trial with each other and perhaps estrangement. There should be a sacred shield around every family.

The home circle should be regarded as a sacred place, a symbol of heaven, a mirror in which to reflect ourselves. Friends and acquaintances, we may have, but in the homelife they are not to meddle. A strong sense of proprietorship should be felt, giving a sense of ease, restfulness, trust." <u>Happiness Homemade,</u> Ellen G. White, pp. 45 – 46.

That's quite a bit to digest. Yet, simply put, when the Sacred Circle is in place – everyone is safe! I know as a new bride, I could not cook. I DID receive some excellent cookbooks, though! Both my mother and my mother-in-law were excellent cooks and their hospitality was renown. I was uncomfortable when each of them came to visit us for the first time, and I kept the meal very simple. Yet, both of them felt it necessary to give instructions on my meal preparation, choice of menu – even how it should be served. I was devastated! Wish we had all known about boundaries then.

Geography gave us a boundary without our even having to try. We began our marriage with a combined 1000 miles between us and either parent. This distance provided us with the opportunity to develop our home and marriage in a way unique to us. It was a combination of what worked in both of our parents' homes and what we felt we could make work for us.

Our first challenge (my husband was a better cook than I was) happened within our first month of marriage. I knew how to prepare dried beans, and since we were on a limited budget, I felt this was something I could do. When I got ready to serve the beans, my husband's first question was

"Where is the rice?" He said in his parent's house, they always had rice with beans, and my response was in my parent's house we never ate rice!

Leaving the home of one's parents often comes down to mealtime! By the way, I have learned to prepare rice and I never serve beans without it!

Here's a visual representation of what the boundaries look like:

Notice, God is always the center of the Christian home. He created husband and wife to be equal in their dominion and authority of their home. Children have a place, but not with the spouses! **EVERYONE** else: parents, siblings, grandparents, aunts, uncles, **and** church members

The Reason Is...

become others! It's what God meant when He said, LEAVE father and mother and become **ONE!** It becomes the work of a lifetime.

Chapter 7

Becoming One

Colossians 3:12-14(MSG)
So, chosen by God for this new life of love, dress in the wardrobe God picked out for you: compassion, kindness, humility, quiet strength, discipline. Be even- tempered, content with second place, quick to forgive an offense. Forgive as quickly and completely as the Master forgave you. And regardless of what else you put on, wear love. It's your basic, all-purpose garment. Never be without it.

The ability to be two independent people who are choosing to be inter-dependent is a hallmark of being prepared for marriage. Too often, people come to a marriage expecting the other person to fill all their needs and make them what they should be. Two whole people should plan to join their lives together and be prepared to stand on their own if need be.

One of the developmental accomplishments of adulthood is to become ***one's own person!*** The societal pressure at the same time is to get married. In spiritual communities, marriage means the **submission** of the woman to the man. Just looking at the expectations: personal, familial, community the personal challenge is to comfortably fit.

A marriage for a lifetime is blessed when both partners have determined **who** they are individually! Popular culture tells young people to find someone who completes them. That's good to write music, but to write a long-lived, successful marriage, each individual should have a sense of completion without another person. It is significant for a person to know who they are, and who they see themselves becoming in the future.

Becoming ONE is a process. The couple who stands before the pastor on their wedding day is not the same couple who celebrates their fifth, seventh, tenth anniversary. People change, and life brings unanticipated challenges, so the marriage changes. One of the qualities needed for a strong marriage is flexibility. Flexibility allows both individuals to grow and change in their personal development.

Our text lets us know that flexibility is necessary. Otherwise, there would be no mention of forgiveness and even-temperedness. Living with a real growing, developing person means that is a need to be flexible. The God Who created us all made us all different – yet we're His masterpiece! (Eph.2:10). Becoming God's masterpiece means when two growing masterpieces come together – there will be rough edges. Compassion, kindness, humility, quiet strength and discipline is needed to facilitate the process.

The additional conundrum for the Christian couple – **submission.** What does that mean? Is the husband the only person in the relationship with an idea, opinion that counts? What is a wife to do when she is a complete adult? I know there is no one answer, but I would like to consider these points.

The Reason Is...

The dictionary defines submission as *the condition of being humble, or compliant.* Being both or either humble or compliant means an individual makes a choice! So, the first characteristic of submission is **personal choice.** If one is made to submit, then that's coercion – a totally different word. Coercion is defined as the use of force or intimidation to obtain compliance. Coercion sounds like domestic abuse to me. The Lord states in Malachi 2:16 (AMP) "For I hate [a]divorce," says the Lord, the God of Israel, "and him who covers his garment with wrong and violence," says the Lord of hosts."

Secondly, the Bible should be read in context. The Scripture often quoted as to the place of women speaks of submission – what's usually left out is the fact that the admonition is for the woman to be submissive to her **own** husband. So, a woman who is single or in a position where other men, not her husband, are involved is not required Biblically, to be submissive.

So, why would a woman choose to submit to her

husband? Here's what Paul says, "Out of respect for Christ, be courteously reverent to one another. Wives, understand and support your husbands in ways that show your support for Christ. The husband provides leadership to his wife the way Christ does to his church, not by domineering but by cherishing. So just as the church submits to Christ as he exercises such leadership, wives should likewise submit to their husbands. Husbands, go all out in your love for your wives, exactly as Christ did for the church—a love marked by giving, not getting. Christ's love makes the church whole. His words evoke her beauty. Everything he does and says is designed to bring the best out of her, dressing her in dazzling white silk, radiant with holiness. And that is how husbands ought to love their wives. They're really doing themselves a favor—since they're already "one" in marriage." **Ephesians 5:21-28 (MSG).**

It's easy to see that becoming one is truly the work of a marriage lifetime. Oneness will not mean always agreeing; acting without thinking; not listening to the voice of God first; forgetting that **Jesus saves** – not one's husband; living in fear; a relationship that reflects God's working in two people to make them in masterpieces. It's scary but exciting. Imagine God being a part of our daily lives in our homes. *"… use your freedom to serve one another in love; that's how freedom grows. For everything we know about God's Word is summed up in a single sentence:* **Love others as you love yourself**.*"* Galatians 5:15 (MSG)

Nothing worth having comes easily. This is a life lesson that I have learned. However, the end product is worth all the struggle. Something like that butterfly: first a caterpillar, then a cocoon, finally a beautiful flying butterfly – after the struggle to free itself from the cocoon. Go ahead, make your marriage a flying butterfly!

Chapter 8

The Journey Continues...

Accept life with humility and patience, making allowances for each other because you love each other. Make it your aim to be at one in the Spirit, and you will inevitably be at peace with one another. You all belong to One body, of which there is one Spirit, just as you all experienced one calling to one hope. Ephesians 4:2-5 (PHILLIPS)

This book does not profess to have all the answers – just to share the joy of the journey of one couple who began over a half century ago! (WOW) It has been a blessing, and it has been one that not's boring. I hope that some of the lessons I have learned will help others as they are on their love journey. I wish for each person reading this that you will laugh and cry as you read and realize

The Reason Is...

that the "best is yet to come!"

I started talking about the four components I thought would create an intimate relationship. They are:

- ♥ **Time**
- ♥ **Commitment**
- ♥ **Humor**
- ♥ **Flexibility**

There is an additional quality that requires all the above to make the journey one of joy, and that is **CHANGE!!!!!** The dictionary defines **Change** as *to become different.* One of the most difficult things for humans to deal with is change! Listen to conversations, *"I wish things were like they used to be. Remember the good old days!"*

Memory has a way of painting the past with soft, glowing colors. It is usually difficult to discern the difficulties of the past. Of course, those who do not develop well can **only** remember the negative experiences of the past.

So, where is the balance? Let's look to the Scriptures: "N*ow every athlete who [goes into training* *and] competes in the games is disciplined and exercises self-control in all things."* **1 Corinthians 9:25 (AMP)** Discipline and self-control are qualities not seen much in today's culture. Maybe because these qualities require a lot of work on a continuous basis, they are not encouraged, valued or sought after. Yet, to enjoy the journey of marriage, self-control and discipline is required. The King James Version of the Bible uses the word temperance.

Let's review those four components through the lens of change. What will temperance do to our world view of marriage? Temperance implies **self-**control. Too many people enter into marriage with a plan to change the **other** person! It is important to remember – **the only person you can change is yourself.** The change that is effective requires the power of the Holy Spirit and the willingness to **surrender** to the will of God. That's a daily, on-going battle – it requires grace for those with whom we're in intimate relationship.

TIME - the one thing that everyone receives an equal amount of. There are only 24 hours in a day for each person. In marriage, there are many time demands. For a marriage to be successful in the journey, the decision must be made to make time for the marriage a priority. Each couple will have to craft the priority for themselves. Yet, without **TIME**, the marriage is challenged for healthy development.

So, what is your decision about **TIME**? It's not the large things – sometimes it comes down to the small things, like the smartphone in your pocket or hand. Just something to consider....

COMMITMENT – This word is not in vogue in today's society. The dictionary defines *commitment* as **the state of being obligated or emotionally impelled.** Since the definition includes a word *impelled*, which is not a part of everyday conversation, it requires definition as well – **impelled** - *to urge or drive forward.* So, commitment includes time – we plan to be married for life, or *"until death do us part."* The plan for commitment involves change.

I am definitely **not** the person I was when I married my husband over 50 years ago! I would like to think that I've improved (smile), but I can say without a doubt I have changed. Our decision to remain married all these years is only possible because we have realized that we both have changed. Change is a part of growth and development and as long as we continue to breathe, we will be subjected to change.

I am so glad commitment was a part of our marriage vows: *"For better, for worse, for richer or poorer, in sickness and in health"*. I have to admit, I didn't realize what those meant on that day, but now I get that change is a part of commitment because we've had all of these qualities across the years. Actually, commitment has helped to make our life exciting – not boring!

HUMOR – Life is serious without a doubt, but we have learned not to take ourselves too seriously! Our ability to see the humor in most of the situations in our marriage has helped us over

The Reason Is...

many a dark patch. We started our marriage in Mississippi in the late 60's. I had never lived in the South; I had no idea what a segregated society looked like. We often walked through the aisles of the Gibson's Discount Store discussing what we **would** buy – if we had money! We would laugh and go home and talk about our exciting evening.

Laughter for us is the foundation of our relationship. We find that we have many things that make us smile, and it has given us the ability to smile at all the changes in our lives. We have moved eight times in our 50+ years of marriage. Sometimes we have even moved in the same city, so the moves have been many. Because we have found something hilarious in all the moves, we find each move a joy and it's a part of our memory bank. Most of the memories are good!

FLEXIBILITY – I have been known as a person who likes control – just a little bit. I guess the hardest lesson for me to learn is that successful change requires compromise. Yet, I have found when I'm willing to see challenges from another point of view – my husband's – we come up with something awesome.

I have also learned change is a part of life, and without flexibility change can break you and the relationship. Our many moves, coupled with children, could have been the death of our marriage. Yet, we have moved, launched successful children, and we're still here looking forward to what's next because we have learned flexibility. Maybe the most important lesson I have learned is control is highly over-rated; it's much more enjoyable to have someone to share life with and we are a formidable team. It's exciting!

Our journey has been a fascinating one. We're not done yet, and I can't wait to see what tomorrow will bring. We're not moving as fast as we used to, but we're still walking together and for that I'm blessed. Hope your journey is as enjoyable as ours.

The Reason Is...

WILMA KIRK LEE
MSW, LCSW

Wilma Kirk-Lee graduated from California State University, Sacramento with a Bachelor of Social Work degree with a concentration in families and children. She received her Master of Social Work from the University of Arkansas Little Rock. She has worked with populations from the aging to early childhood.

She currently directs the ***Center for Family Wholeness***, **(CFW)** located in Houston, Texas. She is one of the founders of the Greater Houston Healthy Marriage Coalition.

Mrs. Kirk-Lee served as Director of Family Ministries of Southwest Region Conference for 12 years along with her husband. She has authored a handbook for family ministries coordinators, *QuickStart for Family Ministries*, at the local church level. She has published a curriculum for marriage called *Marriage Is for Friends*. She also served as a consultant and trainer for the Head Start program in Region Six - Arkansas, Louisiana, New Mexico,

Oklahoma, and Texas.

Mrs. Kirk-Lee has written articles for the *Ministry Magazine, Message, Leadership Magazine, Kids Magazine, The Social NetWorker* and the *Human Sexuality Journal,* a publication for behavioral science college instructors by Williams-Brown Publishing. She has contributed to Sabbath School supplemental books, and she has edited the 2nd edition of the Family Ministries Curriculum and other publications of the Family Ministries department of the North American Division.

Mrs. Kirk Lee was born in Minneapolis, MN to her pastor parents, Augustus L. Kirk and Mildred Bradford Kirk. In 2000, her mother, Mildred Kirk, moved to Houston, Texas to live in proximity. Mrs. Kirk was deceased January 2016.

Wilma has been married to her pastor husband, W. S. Lee for over five decades. She is the mother of three adult children, Anthony, deceased. He left a daughter (Brittany Lee Lineback); she is the mother of Davion and Malik. Adrienne Lee Jones,

The Reason Is...

married to Carl Jones and mother of Samuel Arthur Jones. Amber Lee Williams, married to Christopher Williams, mother of Maxwell Augustus Williams and Miles Christian Williams. Wilma enjoys reading, crocheting, and her love of the color purple is manifested in her daily wardrobe.

www.ingramcontent.com/pod-product-compliance
Lightning Source LLC
Chambersburg PA
CBHW052208110526
44591CB00012B/2128